G000123745

YOU DID IT!

summersdale

YOU DID IT!

An Hachette UK Company
www.hachette.co.uk

Summersdale Publishers Ltd
Part of Octopus Publishing Group Limited
Carmelite House
50 Victoria Embankment
LONDON
EC4Y 0DZ
UK

www.summersdale.com

Printed and bound in China

ISBN: 978-1-78783-529-0

for your Graduation
26TH July 2022

TO Nina Louise
lots of love
FROM Auntie Sue xxx

A winner is a dreamer who never gives up.

NELSON MANDELA

THERE'S NO STOPPING YOU NOW!

WITH DRIVE AND A BIT OF TALENT, YOU CAN MOVE MOUNTAINS.

Dwayne Johnson

We ask ourselves,
who am I to be brilliant,
gorgeous, talented,
and fabulous?
Actually, who are
you not to be?

Marianne Williamson

JUST HOW
FAR CAN
YOU GO?

A HERO IS AN ORDINARY INDIVIDUAL WHO FINDS THE STRENGTH TO PERSEVERE AND ENDURE IN SPITE OF OVERWHELMING OBSTACLES.

Christopher Reeve

The most difficult
thing is the decision
to act, the rest is
merely tenacity.

AMELIA EARHART

YOU CAN
DO ANYTHING
YOU PUT YOUR
MIND TO.

We all have ability.
The difference is how we use it.

STEVIE WONDER

**Believe in yourself
and be strong.**

ADRIANA LIMA

Nice one,
champ!

Giving up
can never ever
be an option.

Greta Thunberg

Follow your inner moonlight; don't hide the madness.

ALLEN GINSBERG

HOW'S THE VIEW FROM THE TOP?

If you cannot
be a poet,
be the poem.

David Carradine

Find out who you are
and do it on purpose.

Dolly Parton

MOUNTAINS
ARE THERE
TO BE
CLIMBED.

MAKE BOLD CHOICES
AND MAKE MISTAKES.
IT'S ALL THOSE THINGS
THAT ADD UP TO THE
PERSON YOU BECOME.

Angelina Jolie

The first step is you have to say that you can.

WILL SMITH

DON'T WAIT FOR OPPORTUNITIES. CREATE THEM.

**Success is something
between you and yourself.
I think only you know where
you've come from and
how far you wanna go.**

RuPaul

I get a satisfaction
from being tested and
defeating the test.

ASHTON EATON

You're on
a roll!

I was taught that the
way of progress was
neither swift nor easy.

Marie Curie

**Genius begins
beautiful works,
but only labour
finishes them.**

JOSEPH JOUBERT

FORGE AHEAD.

THE ARTIST IS
NOTHING WITHOUT
THE GIFT, BUT THE
GIFT IS NOTHING
WITHOUT WORK.

Émile Zola

Do not allow people to dim your shine because they are blinded; tell them to put on some sunglasses.

Lady Gaga

BE YOUR OWN
BIGGEST
CHEERLEADER.

CHAMPIONS ARE MADE
FROM SOMETHING THEY
HAVE DEEP INSIDE THEM –
A DESIRE,
A DREAM,
A VISION.

Muhammad Ali

**Just be yourself
– there is no
one better.**

TAYLOR SWIFT

ENJOY THE FRUITS OF YOUR LABOUR.

Don't give up trying to do
what you really want to do.
Where there is love and
inspiration, I don't think
you can go wrong.

ELLA FITZGERALD

**Success is a science;
if you have the conditions,
you get the result.**

OSCAR WILDE

Be proud of yourself.

There is nothing
impossible to him
who will try.

Alexander the Great

We all start somewhere. It's where you end up that counts.

RIHANNA

BRING
IT ON!

It is not the mountain we conquer, but ourselves.

Edmund Hillary

Celebrate what you've accomplished, but also raise the bar a little higher each time you succeed.

Mia Hamm

DON'T COUNT
THE DAYS.
MAKE THE
DAYS COUNT.

Muhammad Ali

NEVER DOUBT THAT YOU
ARE VALUABLE, POWERFUL,
AND DESERVING OF EVERY
OPPORTUNITY IN THE WORLD
AND EVERY CHANCE TO
PURSUE YOUR OWN DREAMS.

Hillary Clinton

The more
we do,
the more
we can do.

WILLIAM HAZLITT

WHEN
THE GOING
GETS TOUGH,
THE TOUGH
GET GOING.

When you've worked hard,
and done well, and walked
through that doorway of
opportunity, you do not
slam it shut behind you.
You reach back and you give
other folks the same chances
that helped you succeed.

MICHELLE OBAMA

Most people are
paralyzed by fear.
Overcome it and
you take charge of
your life and your world.

MARK VICTOR HANSEN

You're
unstoppable!

The most rewarding
things you do in life
are often the ones
that look like they
cannot be done.

Arnold Palmer

We do not
need magic to
change the world;
we carry all the
power we need
inside ourselves
already.

J. K. ROWLING

THE WORLD IS YOUR OYSTER.

THERE'S NOTHING
MORE INTOXICATING
THAN DOING BIG,
BOLD THINGS.

Jason Kilar

Excellence is not a skill.
It is an attitude.

Ralph Marston

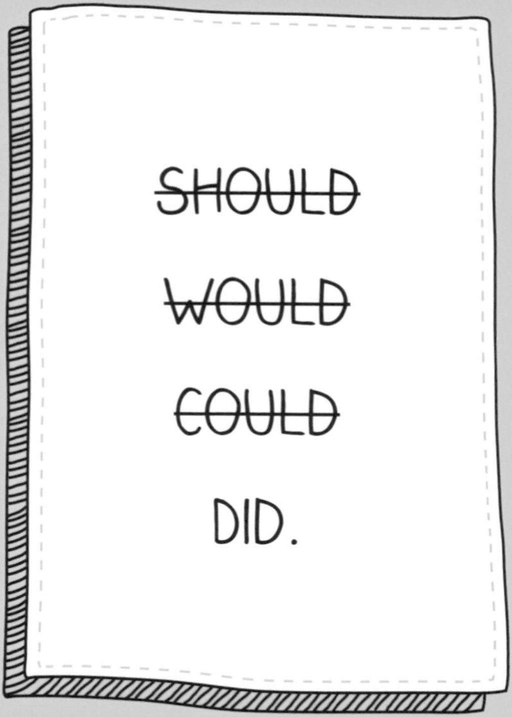
~~SHOULD~~
~~WOULD~~
~~COULD~~
DID.

I THINK LUCK FALLS ON NOT JUST THE BRAVE BUT ALSO THE ONES WHO BELIEVE THEY BELONG THERE.

Novak Djokovic

You deserve to feel good as hell.

LIZZO

I don't like to gamble,
but if there is one thing
I'm willing to bet on,
it's myself.

BEYONCÉ

I still look
at myself and
want to improve.

DAVID BECKHAM

So,
what's
next?

True happiness
comes from the
joy of deeds
well done.

Antoine de Saint-Exupéry

Never give up then, for that's just the place and time that the tide'll turn.

BE

BOLD.

NEVER GIVE UP ON SOMETHING YOU LOVE.

Ariana Grande

Anything is possible
as long as you
keep working at it
and don't back down.

Eminem

YOU MADE
IT HAPPEN.

I AM LUCKY THAT
WHATEVER FEAR
I HAVE INSIDE ME,
MY DESIRE TO WIN IS
ALWAYS STRONGER.

Serena Williams

The right mental
attitude will
bring success
in everything
you undertake.

ELBERT HUBBARD

TOOT YOUR OWN HORN!

A lot of people are afraid
to say what they want.
That's why they don't
get what they want.

MADONNA

**Do your thing
and don't care
if they like it.**

TINA FEY

This is just the beginning.

Life's too short
not to celebrate
nice moments.

Jürgen Klopp

If you're truly passionate about something, you'll make it happen.

LIAM HEMSWORTH

YOU ROCK!

Take your inspiration and let it lead you out into the world, into your big amazing genius life.

Beth Ditto

Everyone can rise
above their
circumstances and
achieve success if they
are dedicated to,
and passionate about,
what they do.

Nelson Mandela

PURSUE
WHAT SETS
YOUR SOUL
ALIGHT.

NEVER SET LIMITS,
GO AFTER YOUR DREAMS,
DON'T BE AFRAID TO
PUSH THE BOUNDARIES.
AND LAUGH A LOT –
IT'S GOOD FOR YOU!

Paula Radcliffe

Accomplishment is something you cannot buy.

ROBERTO CLEMENTE

POSITIVE
THINKING
LEADS TO
POSITIVE
LIVING.

Just remember,
you can do anything
you set your mind to,
but it takes action,
perseverance, and
facing your fears.

GILLIAN ANDERSON

The secret of
success is constancy
of purpose.

BENJAMIN DISRAELI

Your passion propels you.

Never be limited
by other people's
limited imaginations.

Mae Jemison

The greater
the difficulty,
the more glory in
surmounting it.

EPICTETUS

YOU SMASHED IT!

THE QUESTION ISN'T
WHO IS GOING TO
LET ME; IT'S WHO IS
GOING TO STOP ME.

Ayn Rand

Destiny
is not a
matter of chance;
it is a
matter of choice.

William Jennings Bryan

TODAY I WILL
DO WHAT
OTHERS WON'T,
SO TOMORROW,
I CAN DO WHAT
OTHERS CAN'T.

Jerry Rice

LET US PICK UP OUR
BOOKS AND OUR PENS.
THEY ARE OUR MOST
POWERFUL WEAPONS.

Malala Yousafzai

Winning is a habit.

VINCE LOMBARDI

YOUR STORY
IS JUST
GETTING
STARTED.

Nothing splendid has ever been achieved except by those who dared believe that something inside themselves was superior to circumstance.

BRUCE FAIRCHILD BARTON

Happiness is the
consequence of
personal effort.

ELIZABETH GILBERT

Know
your
value.

Dreams do not
come true just because
you dream them.
It's hard work that
makes things happen.
It's hard work that
creates change.

Shonda Rhimes

No great achievement is possible without persistent work.

BERTRAND RUSSELL

SAVOUR THIS MOMENT.

IF YOU HAVE
SOMETHING YOU'RE
REALLY PASSIONATE
ABOUT, DON'T LET
ANYONE TELL YOU THAT
YOU CAN'T DO IT.

Selena Gomez

We are all capable
of awakening and
commitment.
And because of that,
we can all be great.

Alexandria Ocasio-Cortez

TAKE PRIDE IN
HOW FAR YOU
HAVE COME.
HAVE FAITH
IN HOW FAR
YOU CAN GO.

Michael Josephson

NEVER BEND
YOUR HEAD.
ALWAYS HOLD IT HIGH.
LOOK THE WORLD
STRAIGHT IN THE FACE.

Helen Keller

When you are
required to
exhibit strength,
it comes.

JOSEPH CAMPBELL

TRUST, INVEST AND BELIEVE IN YOURSELF.

Stay true to who you are
and what you stand for
and you'll go far in life.

SNOOP DOGG

Life's a climb...
but the view is great.

MILEY CYRUS

Embrace
the
challenge.

Go find your joy.
It's what you're
going to remember
in the end.

Sandra Bullock

Small opportunities are often the beginning of great enterprises.

DEMOSTHENES

LOOK AT
YOU GO!

You should be
free to follow
your star.

Ruth Bader Ginsburg

You have to believe
in the long-term plan
you have, but you need
the short-term goals to
motivate and inspire you.

Roger Federer

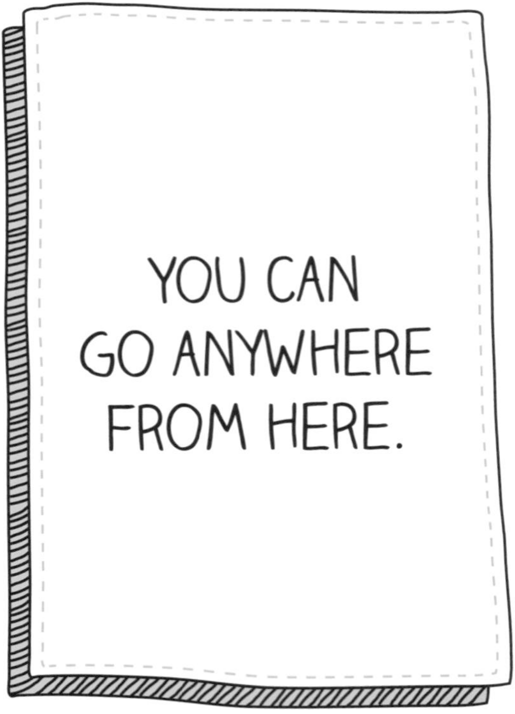
YOU CAN
GO ANYWHERE
FROM HERE.

THE WORLD ALWAYS SEEMS
BRIGHTER WHEN YOU'VE
JUST MADE SOMETHING THAT
WASN'T THERE BEFORE.

Neil Gaiman

What separates
the talented
individual from the
successful one is a
lot of hard work.

STEPHEN KING

THE HARDER THE BATTLE, THE SWEETER THE VICTORY.

Les Brown

It's only when you risk failure that you discover things. When you play it safe, you're not expressing the utmost of your human experience.

LUPITA NYONG'O

If you truly pour your
heart into what you
believe in, even if it
makes you vulnerable,
amazing things can
and will happen.

EMMA WATSON

Let's hear it for you!

Victory is always
possible for the
person who refuses
to stop fighting.

Napoleon Hill

Great difficulties may be surmounted by patience and perseverance.

ABIGAIL ADAMS

YOU DESERVE YOUR SUCCESS.

BELIEF IS THE
IGNITION SWITCH
THAT GETS YOU OFF
THE LAUNCHING PAD.

Denis Waitley

Happiness lies not
in the mere possession
of money; it lies in
the joy of achievement.

Franklin D. Roosevelt

STRIVE
FOR EVEN
GREATER
HEIGHTS.

IF YOU'RE WALKING DOWN
THE RIGHT PATH AND
YOU'RE WILLING TO KEEP
WALKING, EVENTUALLY
YOU'LL MAKE PROGRESS.

Barack Obama

When you
want something,
all the universe
conspires in helping
you to achieve it.

PAULO COELHO

GREAT THINGS DON'T COME FROM COMFORT ZONES.

Roy T. Bennett

Aim at the high mark
and you will hit it.
No, not the first time,
not the second time and
maybe not the third.
But keep on aiming
and keep on shooting...
Finally you'll hit the
bull's-eye of success.

ANNIE OAKLEY

Someone, somewhere,
will say, "Don't do it.
You don't have what it takes
to survive the wilderness."
This is when you
reach deep into your heart
and remind yourself,
"I am the wilderness."

BRENÉ BROWN

Build
on your
success.

Whenever you really
start to believe
in yourself, that's
when it comes to life.

Simone Biles

What you get by
reaching your
goals is not nearly
so important as
what you become
by reaching them.

ZIG ZIGLAR

NEVER GIVE UP.

I'VE REALIZED THAT
OF ALL THE THINGS
I WANTED, MOST OF
THEM WERE AVAILABLE
TO ME ALL ALONG.

Jameela Jamil

The purpose of life...
is to live it, to taste
experience to the
utmost, to reach out
eagerly and without
fear for newer and
richer experience.

Eleanor Roosevelt

THE FUTURE
BELONGS TO
THOSE WHO
BELIEVE IN
THE POWER
OF THEIR
DREAMS.

IF ONE ADVANCES
CONFIDENTLY IN THE
DIRECTION OF HIS DREAMS,
AND ENDEAVOURS TO LIVE
THE LIFE WHICH HE HAS
IMAGINED, HE WILL MEET
WITH A SUCCESS UNEXPECTED
IN COMMON HOURS.

Henry David Thoreau

A happy life
consists not in
the absence, but
in the mastery
of hardships.

HELEN KELLER

DON'T TELL ME THE SKY'S THE LIMIT WHEN THERE ARE FOOTPRINTS ON THE MOON!

Paul Brandt

So many of our dreams at first seem impossible. And then they seem improbable. And then, when we summon the will, they soon become inevitable.

CHRISTOPHER REEVE

Don't try to
lessen yourself
for the world;
let the world
catch up to you.

BEYONCÉ

Show
your
stuff.

You change
the world by
being yourself.

Yoko Ono

Optimism is a faith that leads to success.

BRUCE LEE

DRAW ON YOUR INNER STRENGTH.

ANYTIME SOMEONE
TELLS ME THAT I CAN'T
DO SOMETHING,
I WANT TO DO IT MORE.

Taylor Swift

Pearls don't lie
on the seashore.
If you want one,
you must dive
for it.

Chinese proverb

DON'T
LIMIT YOUR
CHALLENGES.
CHALLENGE
YOUR LIMITS.

Jerry Dunn

SUCCESS IS THE SUM
OF SMALL EFFORTS,
REPEATED DAY IN
AND DAY OUT.

Florence Taylor

With confidence, you have won even before you have started.

MARCUS GARVEY

WITH BIG
DREAMS AND
HARD WORK,
ANYTHING IS
POSSIBLE.

Only those who will risk
going too far can possibly
find out how far one can go.

T. S. ELIOT

The ability to triumph begins with you — always.

OPRAH WINFREY

Find out who
you are and
live that truth.

Ellen DeGeneres

**YOU
DID
IT!**

If you're interested in finding out more about our books, find us on Facebook at **Summersdale Publishers** and follow us on Twitter at **@Summersdale**.

www.summersdale.com